The Story
of
Our Christmas

Christmas is not just a season,
it's a feeling.
It's about family, love,
and the joy that brings us together

this book belongs to:

____

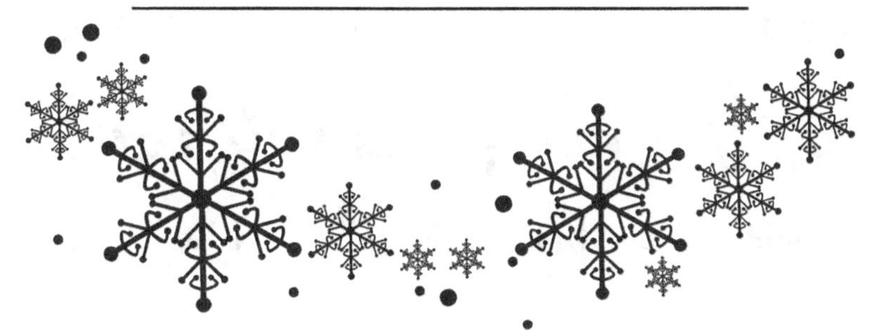

index:

1. The Magic of Christmas

Traditions and Moments That Make the Season Spec

2. Christmas Moments Together

Creating Cherished Memories Through Shared Celebrations

3. Festive Family Recipes

Beloved Family Recipes for a Delicious Holiday Season

1. The Magic of Christmas

Traditions and Moments That Make the Season Spec

Traditions:

Traditions:

Traditions:

Traditions:

Traditions:

Traditions:

Traditions:

Traditions:

Traditions:

Traditions:

Traditions:

Traditions:

Traditions:

Traditions:

Traditions:

Traditions:

Traditions:

Traditions:

Traditions:

Traditions:

Traditions:

Traditions:

Traditions:

Traditions:

Traditions:

Traditions:

Traditions:

Traditions:

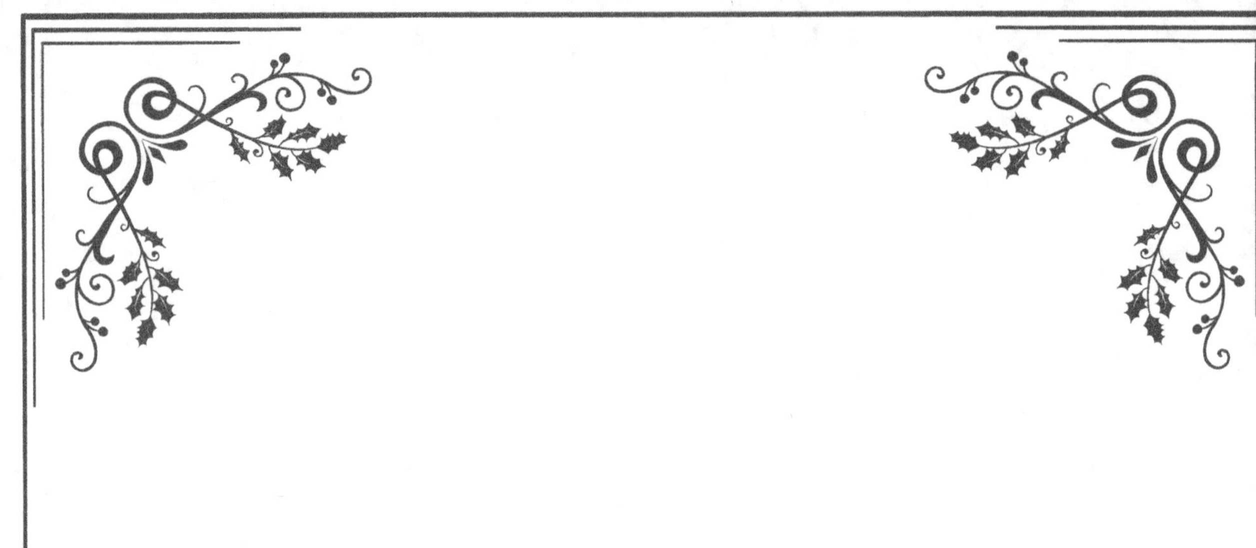

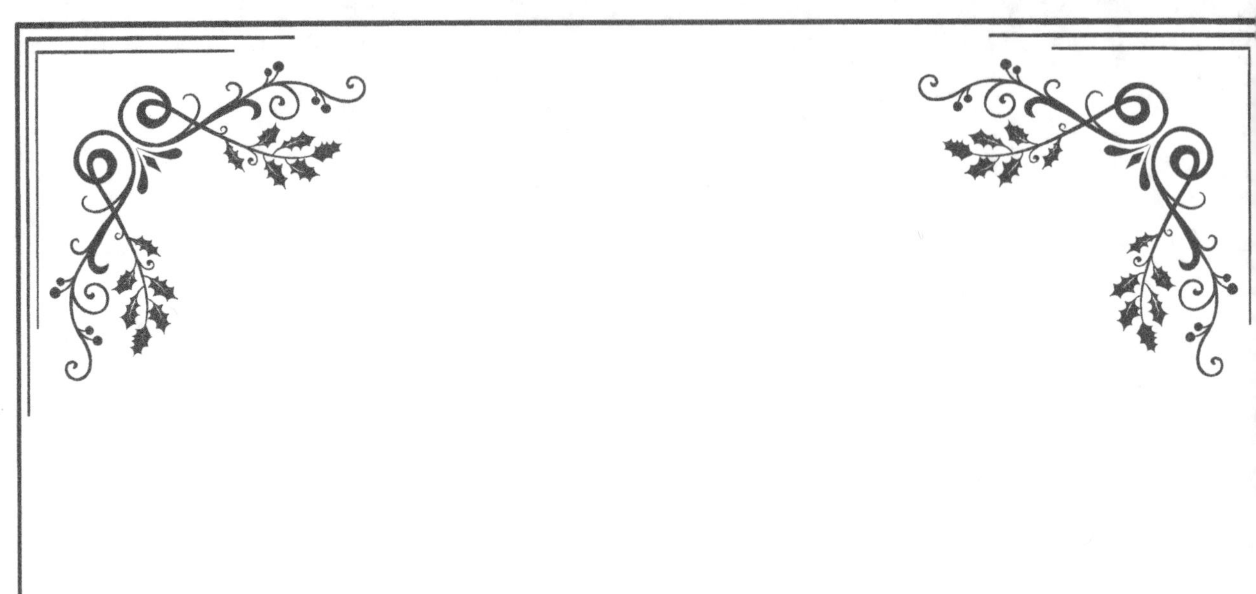

2.Christmas Moments Together

Creating Cherished Memories Through Shared Celebrations

Most memorable Christmas moment this year

The delicious meals and treats enjoyed during This Christmas:

the special moments spent with loved ones

Christmas parties we organized or took part in

Favourite christmas song, movie or web series this year

the holiday decorations and lights that adorned our
surroundings during this Christmas

What we are grateful for:

Attached your photo or card here

Attached your photo or card here

Most memorable Christmas moment this year

The delicious meals and treats enjoyed during This Christmas:

the special moments spent with loved ones

Christmas parties we organized or took part in

Favourite christmas song,movie or web series this year

the holiday decorations and lights that adorned our
surroundings during this Christmas

What we are grateful for:

Attached your photo or card here

Attached your photo or card here

Most memorable Christmas moment this year

The delicious meals and treats enjoyed during This Christmas.

the special moments spent with loved ones

Christmas parties we organized or took part in

Favourite christmas song,movie or web series this year

the holiday decorations and lights that adorned our surroundings during this Christmas

What we are grateful for:

Attached your photo or card here

Attached your photo or card here

Most memorable Christmas moment this year

The delicious meals and treats enjoyed during This Christmas:

the special moments spent with loved ones

Christmas parties we organized or took part in

Favourite christmas song,movie or web series this year

the holiday decorations and lights that adorned our
surroundings during this Christmas

What we are grateful for:

Attached your photo or card here

Attached your photo or card here

Most memorable Christmas moment this year

The delicious meals and treats enjoyed during This Christmas:

the special moments spent with loved ones

Christmas parties we organized or took part in

Favourite christmas song,movie or web series this year

the holiday decorations and lights that adorned our
surroundings during this Christmas

What we are grateful for:

Attached your photo or card here

Attached your photo or card here

Most memorable Christmas moment this year

The delicious meals and treats enjoyed during This Christmas:

the special moments spent with loved ones

Christmas parties we organized or took part in

Favourite christmas song,movie or web series this year

the holiday decorations and lights that adorned our
surroundings during this Christmas

What we are grateful for:

Attached your photo or card here

Attached your photo or card here

Most memorable Christmas moment this year

The delicious meals and treats enjoyed during This Christmas:

the special moments spent with loved ones

Christmas parties we organized or took part in

Favourite christmas song,movie or web series this year

the holiday decorations and lights that adorned our
surroundings during this Christmas

What we are grateful for:

Attached your photo or card here

Attached your photo or card here

Most memorable Christmas moment this year

The delicious meals and treats enjoyed during This Christmas:

the special moments spent with loved ones

Christmas parties we organized or took part in

Favourite christmas song,movie or web series this year

the holiday decorations and lights that adorned our
surroundings during this Christmas

What we are grateful for:

Attached your photo or card here

Attached your photo or card here

Most memorable Christmas moment this year

The delicious meals and treats enjoyed during This Christmas:

the special moments spent with loved ones

Christmas parties we organized or took part in

Favourite christmas song, movie or web series this year

the holiday decorations and lights that adorned our
surroundings during this Christmas

What we are grateful for:

Attached your photo or card here

Attached your photo or card here

Most memorable Christmas moment this year

The delicious meals and treats enjoyed during This Christmas:

the special moments spent with loved ones

Christmas parties we organized or took part in

Favourite christmas song,movie or web series this year

the holiday decorations and lights that adorned our
surroundings during this Christmas

What we are grateful for:

Attached your photo or card here

Attached your photo or card here

3. Festive Family Recipes

Beloved Family Recipes for a Delicious Holiday Season

Recipe Card

DIFFICULTY

NAME OF DISH

INGREDIENTS:

PREP TIME:

COOK TIME:

SERVES:

DIRECTIONS:

MEMORIES:

Recipe Card

○ ○ ○ ○ ○
DIFFICULTY

NAME OF DISH

INGREDIENTS:

PREP TIME:

COOK TIME:

SERVES:

DIRECTIONS:

MEMORIES:

Recipe Card

DIFFICULTY

NAME OF DISH

INGREDIENTS:

PREP TIME:

COOK TIME:

SERVES:

DIRECTIONS:

MEMORIES:

Recipe Card

DIFFICULTY

NAME OF DISH

INGREDIENTS:

PREP TIME:

COOK TIME:

SERVES:

DIRECTIONS:

MEMORIES:

Recipe Card

DIFFICULTY

NAME OF DISH

INGREDIENTS:

PREP TIME:

COOK TIME:

SERVES:

DIRECTIONS:

MEMORIES:

Recipe Card

○ ○ ○ ○ ○

DIFFICULTY

NAME OF DISH

INGREDIENTS:

PREP TIME:

COOK TIME:

SERVES:

DIRECTIONS:

MEMORIES:

Recipe Card

○ ○ ○ ○ ○
DIFFICULTY

NAME OF DISH

INGREDIENTS:

PREP TIME:

COOK TIME:

SERVES:

DIRECTIONS:

MEMORIES:

Recipe Card

NAME OF DISH

INGREDIENTS:

PREP TIME:

COOK TIME:

SERVES:

DIRECTIONS:

MEMORIES:

Recipe Card

DIFFICULTY

NAME OF DISH

INGREDIENTS:

PREP TIME:

COOK TIME:

SERVES:

DIRECTIONS:

MEMORIES:

Recipe Card

○ ○ ○ ○ ○
DIFFICULTY

NAME OF DISH

INGREDIENTS:

PREP TIME:

COOK TIME:

SERVES:

DIRECTIONS:

MEMORIES:

Recipe Card

DIFFICULTY

NAME OF DISH

INGREDIENTS:

PREP TIME:

COOK TIME:

SERVES:

DIRECTIONS:

MEMORIES:

Recipe Card

DIFFICULTY

NAME OF DISH

INGREDIENTS:

PREP TIME:

COOK TIME:

SERVES:

DIRECTIONS:

MEMORIES:

Recipe Card

○ ○ ○ ○ ○
DIFFICULTY

NAME OF DISH

INGREDIENTS:

-
-
-
-
-
-

-
-
-
-
-
-

PREP TIME:

COOK TIME:

SERVES:

DIRECTIONS:

MEMORIES:

Recipe Card

DIFFICULTY

NAME OF DISH

INGREDIENTS:

PREP TIME:

COOK TIME:

SERVES:

DIRECTIONS:

MEMORIES:

Recipe Card

○ ○ ○ ○ ○
DIFFICULTY

NAME OF DISH

INGREDIENTS:

PREP TIME:

COOK TIME:

SERVES:

DIRECTIONS:

MEMORIES:

Recipe Card

DIFFICULTY

NAME OF DISH

INGREDIENTS:

PREP TIME:

COOK TIME:

SERVES:

DIRECTIONS:

MEMORIES:

Recipe Card

DIFFICULTY

NAME OF DISH

INGREDIENTS:

PREP TIME:

COOK TIME:

SERVES:

DIRECTIONS:

MEMORIES:

Recipe Card

DIFFICULTY

NAME OF DISH

INGREDIENTS:

PREP TIME:

COOK TIME:

SERVES:

DIRECTIONS:

MEMORIES:

Recipe Card

○ ○ ○ ○ ○

DIFFICULTY

NAME OF DISH

INGREDIENTS:

PREP TIME:

COOK TIME:

SERVES:

DIRECTIONS:

MEMORIES:

Recipe Card

○ ○ ○ ○ ○
DIFFICULTY

NAME OF DISH

INGREDIENTS:

PREP TIME:

COOK TIME:

SERVES:

DIRECTIONS:

MEMORIES:

Recipe Card

DIFFICULTY

NAME OF DISH

INGREDIENTS:

PREP TIME:

COOK TIME:

SERVES:

DIRECTIONS:

MEMORIES:

Recipe Card

○ ○ ○ ○ ○
DIFFICULTY

NAME OF DISH

INGREDIENTS:

-
-
-
-
-
-

-
-
-
-
-
-

PREP TIME:

COOK TIME:

SERVES:

DIRECTIONS:

MEMORIES:

Recipe Card

DIFFICULTY

NAME OF DISH

INGREDIENTS:

PREP TIME:

COOK TIME:

SERVES:

DIRECTIONS:

MEMORIES:

Recipe Card

○ ○ ○ ○ ○

DIFFICULTY

NAME OF DISH

INGREDIENTS:

PREP TIME:

COOK TIME:

SERVES:

DIRECTIONS:

MEMORIES: